A Square of Sunlight

A Square of Sunlight

Meg Cox

smith|doorstop

the poetry business

Published 2021 by The Poetry Business
Campo House,
54 Campo Lane,
Sheffield S1 2EG
www.poetrybusiness.co.uk

Designed & typeset by The Poetry Business.
Printed by Imprint Digital.
Cover Painting: *Together* by Rose Arbuthnott (rosearbuthnottartist.co.uk)

British Library Cataloguing-in-Publication Data.
A catalogue record for this book is available from the British Library.

Smith|Doorstop is a member of Inpress
www.inpressbooks.co.uk.
Distributed by NBN International, 1 Deltic Avenue,
Rooksley, Milton Keynes MK13 8LD.

The Poetry Business gratefully acknowledges the support
of Arts Council England.

Contents

For Deborah Alma
poet, generous mentor and loved friend

A Square of Sunlight

She dawdled home as usual through the town
with school friends. One was left at the station
another at the library. Three of them stopped
at the bakers in the High Street for free stale cakes
and after some window shopping by the time
she reached the Butter Cross she was on her own.
She turned into the Close and took the short cut
through the Cathedral, in the front and out the back,
touching the Jane Austen grave, then hurrying
under St Swithuns church, into Kingsgate Street,
through the garage to the front door at the back
under the scent of ripening pears against the wall.
The hall, shadowy dining room and its candle smell,
through the breakfast room, by the walk-in larder,
shedding satchel, blazer, boater and shoes as she went
into the kitchen, back door open, and her dad
in his cricket whites, prone and beating his fist
on the quarry tiled floor in a square of sunlight.

The Law of Unintended Consequences

I blame my mother.
Aged four I ran home
from school to tell her
my new word 'fuck'.
I didn't say it twice.
She said she didn't
even like to think it,
let alone speak it
and it was a very,
very naughty word.

I said it a lot after that:
in my bedroom
under the bedclothes
savouring its sinful sound,
and aloud when alone
walking the dog
in the water meadows,
practising for my future.

Stan

Cricket Field Road in Horsham
was where I went once a week
for piano lessons with
the village organist, a family friend.

I can remember walking
along that road admiring my feet
in new Clarks sandals
but few other memories.

I do remember a metronome on the top
of the shiny black upright piano
and Stan's shiny black hair.

I would remember more
but luckily for me Stan liked to play
with little boys and not little girls.

'She was the kind of person who keeps a parrot'

Mark Twain

Welsh probably. She wore a hand-knitted grey cardigan,
and a Celtic knot brooch, most of the time.
Brought up by elderly Edwardian parents
in the thickly painted green and brown villa
(brother died in the second world war)
she saw them to their graves, slowly and willingly.
The Townswomen's Guild wouldn't have been
the same without her scones.
The elderly cat foisted on her after the funeral
by the local vicar didn't suit and didn't last.

But then she got Bertie for company.
He was a fabulously riotous, flapping, feathered,
blue, red and yellow fluster of beak and claw,
coarse voiced, free minded, friendly, crapping,
indiscriminate glory of a bird. *Take yer knickers off, darlin'*
the milkman heard the bird say. That's what I know about her.

Showing Promise

When my father was sixteen
he could throw an egg over the house,
run through the rooms
and catch the egg unbroken
in the back garden.
The doors would be open,
his mother in the kitchen
sighing *oh George* as he dashed
and his dad outside
nodding but keeping one eye
on his cabbages –
showing off

The Best Medicine

It must be genetic
that just lying on our backs
made me and my brother laugh.
When we had adjoining bedrooms
our mother would shout up the stairs
stop reading now and go to sleep.
Later she would shout again
stop laughing now.

Adult, I went to yoga classes
and at the end we had to lie
on our backs on our mats and relax
doing yogic breathing but before long
I was asked to leave before that part –
disruptive to meditation.

Come to think of it
lying on my back laughing
has caused me quite a bit of trouble
in the past.

Aldermaston March 1962

I was the dissenter.
I was the one who walked fifty miles
with thousands of others
slept on hard floors
carried a sleeping bag
and four pairs of spare knickers.
I was the one who hardly got to clean my teeth
and peed behind bushes.
I was Joan of Arc
fighting to 'Ban the Bomb'
for the good of the world.
And for Paul the college friend I fancied,
who pleaded with me to do the walk
with him but after the first day
when I opposed his plans
for how we'd sleep, he quickly
got into another girl's sleeping bag,
one which was next to mine
on a smelly village school floor.

1963

The house is in Chatou, a southwest suburb of Paris.
It has proper French tree lined streets and stag beetles
noisily hovering under a fretted iron street lamp.
The kitchen is three times the size of our kitchen,
and foreign, hung with paintings. There are three windows
all without mullions but they aren't doors.
It's dark outside and I'm alone in the house, sitting
on the scrubbed pine table with my bare feet up on the dresser
because I'm painting my toe nails and drinking real coffee.

My book *Bonjour Tristesse* (in French) is open beside me.
I've turned on the radio hoping to hear the Beatles' first LP.
There's some Bach. I fiddle with the dial.
After more solemn music an announcement
Le Président Kennedy est mort.
Above the radio is a sketch of a sparrow by Picasso on a red
          mount.
I know now it wasn't an original.
I was kissed by a Frenchman the week before.
I am 19 and this is just the beginning of my life.

Second Person Personal

It must have been around dusk
when you were strolling home
the last half mile from the tube
along empty Willesden streets
the plane trees glowing green
with a blackbird mistaking
the street lights for day
and singing loudly above you
that you think
you are being followed
and you pick up speed
but when the stalker shuffles his feet
too close behind you
you swing round and shout at him
you should know better
and *how dare you*
and *I know where you live*
you bastard!

Break

In a side ward, twelve young men
each with a fractured leg or two in traction.
Most were bikers – this was Brighton
at the time of Mods and Rockers,
their sweaty leathers in their lockers.
They were fit, bored and helpless.

As I went in with my bowl of hot soapy water
the ward would ring with wolf whistles,
cheers and jeers. Bed-bath time.
No curtains so a running commentary
on the state of each man's erection.
The ward sister would take her tea break.

Very Small Italians

The first time I had sex in a car
it was in a Fiat 600 and I'm not short.
Me and my friend paid twenty quid
each to go to Rimini on a coach
and we met these Italian men
(and we saw Gina Lollobrigida in a café)
and one of these Italian men
had a very tiny car and he and I
had a very uncomfortable shag.
Only the once and never again.

Ah Yes I Remember It Well

After Alan J Lerner and Frederick Loewe

You phoned and said *meet me in Paris*.
I can only remember that I got there in half a day.
It was very cold, we agreed on that at least.

You say there was no escalator at Orly in 1970
but I can remember sinking down on it
looking for and finding you in the crowd.

Even if there were no escalator
I do remember that sinking feeling
of seeing you in your black polo neck

and your face changing when you saw me
which was the beginning of falling in love.

Flat Lands

We didn't intend visiting Aigues Mortes
on our drift around the South of France,
swimming in the Med, visiting museums.
We were camping with all we needed
in the back of our open Golf GTI,
moving on every day. September,
almost the vendange. Moules. Ripe fruit.
Garlic and tomatoes fried over the Gaz
with oil and french bread. Sex.

And then Aigues Mortes stopped us.
What was that? The name, the flat lands?
It was a hard place, old and dangerous
it seemed to us. We weren't welcome.
I wanted to see the horses of the Carmague
but it was closed. Coarse windswept grass.
Salt dead water, not the warm Mediterranean
but a grey stone and defended edge land, different.
I remember mostly the wild horses
we didn't see, tossing their manes.

Sometimes It's a Quiet Poem

like the sweep
of the willow in the wind
beyond the hedge

or the movement
of the tail of my dog
when I smile

it could be
a petal falling from the jug
of yellow tulips

or the snow
on the window after dark
rain on a pond

the ember
that falls in the log burner
behind the glass

it might be
the last sight of him at the corner
when he didn't look back

or a cloud covering the sun.

The Next Holiday

All night through my open window
the garrulous sea calls and grumbles
against the pebbled shore.
Early I walk to the sea.

I take our old way, through rough grasses
that scratch my hands and bare legs,
rather than the longer track,
the deep smuggler's route.

Briefly the great scoop of the bay
reveals itself, the salient black rocks
and the empty harbour. I plunge
steeply to our secret entrance

and step alone onto the beach.
The risen sun blinds me, sky and sea
blur into iridescence, the lost sound
of your laughter deafens me.

Tourists

When I remember Florence
it is not the Ponte Vecchio
but the narrow singing streets
where we looked for a laundrette
holding hands.

The Third Person in the Marriage

The bastard's just left; walked out just now,
he's gone back to her – that effing old cow.
He packed all his stuff and he wouldn't say why,
walked out of the door without a goodbye.
He said that she bored him, he said he loved me,
but she's got his children, and I'm forty three.
I just don't get it, she's such a doormat,
he says she's 'clever'. Read 'fat'.
I'll get you back. Watch me strut my stuff,
I've got tits to die for, wear Chanel in the buff.
You said we were finished. But that can't be true –
it can't be too late for us – I really love you.
And what has she got, that woman, I've not?
Just his kids, a house, my lover. The lot.

Europe

Once upon a time I loved you more than apple orchards
in spring when the blossom was heavy with bees,
more than the South Downs on my horizon
and more than pizza in Sienna on the steps
of the Piazza del Campo in September.
I loved you more than the Van Gogh Museum
and petit déjeuner outside a café in Arle
or reaching the Mediterranean, taking off our clothes
and running into the sea.
I loved you more than the whole of Symi
and the City of London seen from Tate Modern,
more than sardines cooked on a Portuguese beach,
more than *Henry V*, more even than Larkin at his best.
I can't say more than that. That's got to be enough.

Awake at Night

listening to the World Service
(one benefit of sleeping on my own)
I heard a man explain he wasn't lonely;
he talked to his dead wife all the time
although he knew she wasn't there.

He told her about things she would once
have liked, and still did, according to him.
He asked her advice about the children
but didn't say if what she said was any help.

As I drifted off to sleep I wondered
if I could do that too – talk to him.
But when your own dear departed
is still living with his wife in Wembley
it's just not the same.

Cadeau

I must get on with the ironing,
the last of the pile from a week ago
which hasn't been done yet, my dear,
because of all that has happened.
Although you took some of your clothes
your best shirts were in the wash
ready for me to press for you as usual.
I have borrowed an iron from Man Ray
(you know the one? studded with spikes).
He believed in making the useful
useless which reminded me of you.
So I am using his iron for your shirts.
And they will be ready for you, my dear,
should you return to collect them.

Recollected in Herefordshire

It was the third time I'd been to Tate Modern
and never been up to the restaurant.
We'd seen the Ai WeiWei sunflower seeds
in the Turbine Hall and trailed round the shop.
Then to the sixth floor to have a sit
and 'wild mushroom and baby spinach pastry case
with a poached duck egg' which was perfect.
The day, which had been overcastish,
cleared as we finished our wine and the sun
came out on Wordsworth's fair city,
more beautiful than anything seen before –
St Paul's, the Thames, other towers and temples.
We had some coffee and I fell in love again.

Nightingales

I heard someone say there were nightingales
in the woods where I am staying
in the South of France.
I haven't heard them.

In fact I may not have heard what was said,
by the person who wasn't talking to me but
to someone else who I think said that
they hadn't heard them either.

So at least if they are singing in the trees
where I am staying in the South of France
I am not the only person
not to have heard them.

But I did hear your voice yesterday
in the next room, although you're not here.
Perhaps tonight I will hear the nightingales
and your voice. In my dreams.

L'esprit de l'escalier

I used to laugh at my brother
who talked to himself, silent
but moving his lips, and I knew
he was going over meetings
and conversations
thinking up responses
he didn't make at the time.
We all do it and some languages
have a word or phrase for it.
I don't think I've done it much
but I would like to have thought
of something I could have said
to my brother before it was too late.

'a boy falling out of the sky'

(W H Auden)

In the case of my brother
it was men's desultory talk outside the curtains
How'd you get 'ere? Ambulance?
Inside, the laboured breathing
into a mask and a kind of silence.
Through the windows looking down
from high over Hampstead
it was an afternoon in December,
the festive lights lit as the day darkened.
The shoppers, the taxis, the rain.
I come by bus. Forgot me teeth.
I could have been down there
buying presents, Christmas cards,
having a coffee, a bit cross, looking at my list.
I could have bought him something
he might have liked.

I'll Never Again

do long jump on the village cricket ground
into the hill of hot grass cuttings and win,
walk over the Downs until we can see the sea,
climb the trees in Winchester College playing fields
or wade in gumboots through the water meadows with our dog,
cycle to work from Willesden Green to Chelsea,
walk the Mortimer Trail in two days
(but the opposite way from the guidebook –
all the signs pointing backwards),
see The Seated Man and the view he sees
from above Castleton in the North York Moors,
walk out of Rome on the dusty Appian Way
to eat al fresco in a restaurant – a pink cotton napkin
and a wisteria blossom placed on my plate.
I'll never run up stairs, run down, two at a time, again
or live in a flat with a view, unless it has a lift.
I still have the pink napkin.

Near Ypres

It wasn't the lecture from the guide
on the terrible waste and the mud
and it wasn't the beat of the marching feet
parading at the Menin Gate
nor the flashing noisy museum
with its modelled and photographed dead.

It was the numbers and the names
on the white stones in rows
under the open innocent sky.
It was the tended planted fields,
the hedges and the travellers' joy.
It was the wind moving the sweep
of the young willows.
It was the quiet that made me weep.

Today's Headlines

I was sitting next to the wood burner,
keeping warm, thinking about things,
like the snow, the spring, the news
of 300 circus fleas dead of cold somewhere.
They were doing OK, a regular job,
regular food, learning a trade.
Then they died of neglect.
None of us deserve that,
to be unfound at your stairs' foot,
dumped in a ditch, forgotten in a
cold house or trapped in a box
left outside in the cold,
when you are only doing your best
in the one chance you have of a life.

LBJs

Driving home from Sussex I turned off the M4
at the large roundabout near Swindon –
stationary at the lights there was sudden peace
after the motorway. I was close to the island,
green with trees and shrubs, where small birds
darted over the cars and into the leaves.
Despite the thrum of my engine and
the whoosh of the rushing lorries below
I could hear the clamorous cheeping
of nestlings demanding food. They were
so close but so distant from my life.
The lights changed and I drove on,
my mind no longer full of death and memories
but half full of something almost like hope.

Impressions of Jordan from a Car

The satisfaction of seeing four camels
aloofly folded and Bedouin rugged
on wasteland between
modern blocks of flats.

Common or garden black plastic bag birds
kept hovering over the highway
by the fierce sandy updrafts
from tankers of oil or water.

Wrinkled bare dun cliffs below
cascading houses necklaced
by sun-sparkled household cans,
bottles and more plastic.

Distant desert rocks like grazing sheep,
a tree against the hotel shaking
with late chattering birds,
dirty underskirts of palms.

Brown road signs to Petra and Wadi Rum,
blue signs to working towns,
warning signs to the Syrian border
the greening of the desert with refugee tents.

Remember This

Just our usual walk to the tube,
me and my Labrador in the rain.
We were both wet by the time
we got to The Royal Court Theatre.

The lights of the shops shone
from the gutters and puddles,
taxis were queuing at the rank
but the theatre lights weren't yet up.

A woman in a headscarf
and hunched into a trench coat
hurried from the dark stage door
but bent to pat my dog, Rick.

What's your name? she said to him
but before I could introduce him to Ingrid
she said *Beautiful*, smiled at me,
turned and walked away.

We stood silently and watched her
climb into the plane (I mean taxi)
and she was gone, forever.
But she and Rick will always have Sloane Square.

Dear Frank O'Hara

I am writing this to you because
you are dead. I was in Leominster
and you know how sometimes
you remember exactly where
you were when something happened
like the death of JFK, it was like that.
It was hot and I was in a hurry
but had to stand and watch
the fire brigade stop all the traffic
to put up a ladder and rescue
a bird from the spire of the church
next to the library and that
reminded me that I had read
just one of your poems in an anthology
and meant to read more
so I trotted into the library and found
out that you had died twenty years ago.
I had to sit down. The bird flew away.

Strawberries

Twisting old newspapers
to light the wood burner
and rereading bits, I found a poem
which I tore out, about strawberries,
or anyway about love, by Edwin Morgan,
illumined by luscious descriptions
of lustfully shared fruit in the sunshine.
I read it twice
and I could taste the fruit and you.
We were in the garden in the heat,
the juice of a glut of ripe strawberries
being shared between us.
And for that moment, kneeling
by the unlit fire, it was summer.

Argos

I'm very tired now. I'm old and I ache in every leg.
I've been lying out here where I can see the sea road
from the shade of the fig tree she planted for me years ago.

Before my master left we used to go hunting,
kings of our world. *Wait for me*, he said.
I'm going to win a war. I'll be back soon.
Look after her for me.

His hand on my head, his voice in my ears
all these years. Days ago something changed
in the air, in the smell, a shiver in my spine –
he's coming. She knows. I will sleep soon.

Bird of Prey

The first time I saw him
at the local petting farm
he was venting his frustration
on some gumboots left outside
the tea room door
because when he was younger
he was allowed in
to take cake from the visitors
oohing and *aahing*.
He was bigger than I expected,
more than knee high,
a fat puff of grey feather,
big eyed, skin and bone.
On later visits he was tethered
on a stand – *Do not feed the owl*.
Swivelling to the visitors' touch,
his mind was as usual
on the titbits he wasn't being given.
Then it was the old cages at the back
on his own – *This bird is dangerous*.
Given half a bloody chance.

Brief Encounter

I step through the front door
to a sound like a shot – Bang!
On the path four feet away
the buzzard hits the ground
on its feet, missed its prey.
Our hearts stop, our eyes lock
for one long second
before he is sucked into the sky, gone.

The stare of him.

Cowlick

It's a long journey alone
and then a halt at roadworks.
To my right near the fence
is a group of cattle and their calves.
One cow is licking her calf's ear,
thoroughly and roughly,
and the calf's head is turned
to one side, reluctant but compliant
and I recognise my mother
washing my ears and behind my ears
and my head turned at just that angle
with a flannel as coarse as a cow's tongue.

Never Mind D H Lawrence

Swallows? Never mind swallows,
it's swifts, they're the boys
sweeping and screeching through the evening sky
chasing and calling,
looping and weaving way out of sight.

Star Wars? Never mind *Star Wars*.
It's swifts, they're the ones.
Never such aerodynamics, such flying in formation,
dive bombing buildings, near misses to make a pilot weep,
and away, screaming and calling, knowing.

Martins? Never mind martins,
it's swifts, they're the birds.
Stand near the house on a summer evening and those distant
         dots
In the blue distance turn, nearer and lower and whoosh,
over your head, laughing.

Swifts, they're the boys.

Wearing Purple

after Jenny Joseph

Now that I am an old woman I shall
sit on a bench at the seaside
with four other old women
that I don't like and one old man at the end.
We'll have a cake in a tea room
and be home on the bus before *Corrie*.
We'd never miss *Antiques Roadshow*
of course, that's our heritage.

Now that I'm an old woman I might
treat myself to one of those electric chairs
with a footrest and my neighbour says
that some of them tip you out as well.
I don't need a stair lift unfortunately because
I live in a bungalow but I do wonder
how much those walk-in baths cost.
I don't believe in showers.

Now that I'm an old woman I will
wear pastels, which are very nice,
mostly from Marks & Spencer.
My old mother used to say she liked
'cardigan weather' which was when
it was nice and sunny but a cardi
was cosy and kept your arms covered
and now I know what she meant.

Red Tulips

On the kitchen table
for ten days now
easing themselves into old age
before they drop and die
red tulips glow
day by day
spread and droop
more graceful
than new stiffly upright
blooms tight and fresh
a youth they can't recover
but beautiful as they bend
and fade, shine dulled
exposing their hearts
as they near their end
each head held upwards.

Déjà Vu at the Surgery

My GP is a kind and busy man
and that flick of his eyes
to the wall clock
caught as I look up
was intended to be discreet.
He isn't to know
how practiced I am
at keeping my eye
on the lightning glance
of a man who needs
to watch the time
without my knowing.

Just When You Thought You Were Safe

grief jumps out at you from a cupboard
in the shed you've never used,
full of worn gardening and walking clothes
kept separate because they're dirty

and just as you turn the corner
onto your street thinking how lovely
it will be to get home, take your shoes off
and share a glass of red wine.

And when you are sitting in the very last
waiting area that you've moved into from
two other last waiting areas at Heathrow,
it's waiting to check your boarding pass.

It is even on page 54 of the book
you took with you to read on the beach.

Five a Day

Poking through hard imported fruit,
untempted,
I remember a distant summer
where green and black figs
squashed by their own ripe weight
in a wet brown paper bag
are lying on the grass in the shade
near an empty bottle of wine,
the picnic rug where we are lying
half naked, sated.

Excuse me
a metallic nudge against
my empty trolley –
I am standing on my own,
middle aged, in Morrisons,
in March, in the Midlands.

Woman's Hour

Doing some ironing one morning
I found myself listening to an interesting talk
about slim line tracksuit bottoms
but that worried me because
I knew they wouldn't suit my bottom.
After I'd learnt some useful uses
for reusable plastic bags
I listened to some women talking
about their elective labial reduction surgery –
'correct and define your inner labia'.
Unlike those other parts of my body
I have spent my life worrying about,
my bottom (see above), and my nose, and my knees,
I thought 'that part' had served me well,
and anyway ... But it seemed clear
that my life might be improved, even now,
by such an up-to-date fashionable piece of equipment.
Maybe nothing would be finer than a designer vagina.

Faithless

If I had seen him on the water
walking on the water I mean
and seen the hem of his robe
darkening and dragging,
and his sandals heavy and slippery
(unless he took them off before
stepping carefully onto
the nervous skin of the Sea)
and the waves backing off
like friendly dogs told to *get down*
and the dark clouds clapping
the man lime-lit by lightning

I might have believed.

Not So Much

I like unexpected hugs from warm men
but air kisses from women, not so much.
I love dogs and I do like cats
just not quite as much.
I used to like living in London but then
I moved and I don't like the country so much.
I like temperate climates, not hot weather as much.
Books are best but not magazines so much.
I do quite like the word 'much'
but I really don't like being so opinionated.

Mismatch

I was only the French Maid now and again
in a little black dress, stockings and duster.
She was 'Brigitte' and I couldn't do the accent.
I'd have liked to be any Bond girl
with a name like Trigger or Vesper or Solitaire,
or even Ursula Undress with a knife.
But I was Miss Jones instead, twinset and pearls
and glasses to remove, revealing my beauty,
Miss Jones I had no idea you were ...
She was easier, although I wasn't convincing
apparently.

But now I can take part with my eyes shut.
He and I can be doctor and patient –
me lying in bed in a hospital gown and a coma
and he Sir Lancelot Spratt come on his rounds
to give me a poke. And that almost suits us both.

Ode to my Bosch SPS 20/24

with apologies to EBB

How do I love you? Let me count the ways.
I love you for your depth and breadth and height
and yet for fitting tight below the worktop.
When you've done your work and Bolognese
is no longer awfully sticky hard and crusty,
I love you. Or when you're full of china,
saucepans, knives and forks and finer
painted ware to boil, ungrease, and dusty
ornaments to benefit from soda, I love you.
I love you when you're full but everything
on your shelves is washed and dry and sparkling.
I love you empty, ready to load all over.
You're my whizzbang clean, you're my always pristine,
beloved and faithful, you're my favourite machine.

Sea Fever

with apologies to John Masefield

I must go down to the beach again to the crowded beach
      and the sand,
where all I need is a big towel, my bikini and a man's hand
to help me down and help me up and smooth on the factor
      sixty,
when the sun is hot and there is no shade and we are mostly
      tipsy.

I must go down to the beach again for the call of the
      ice-cream van
is a loud tune and an old tune and the cornets are all
      gargantuan,
and all I ask is some fish and chips and the sound of the
      children whooping
as they wee in the sea and kick the sand at the greedy
      sea-gulls swooping.

I must go down to the beach again for a walk on the
      fretwork pier,
for the Punch and Judy, the slot machines and another
      bottle of beer.
Then all I ask is a bit of a snooze and a sit on the promenade
with a friend off the bus and time to write you a
      wish-you-were-here postcard.

One Reason to Go Out When It's Raining

In December there were no cars
by the bridge over the river Arrow
where families stop in summer to picnic and paddle

just a white BT van on the puddled mud.
I slowed down and saw a man
on the grass beside the river.

He was wearing wet weather gear,
work boots and a hard hat
and he was playing
with a very small black dog.

The green field, thin trees
and grey sky. The big man
and his puppy running
and dancing together.

I didn't stop to watch because
I was late and it wasn't much
but it made me smile
as I drove on over the bridge.

Brian

Last week I rescued a lump of moss
which had fallen from the roof,
and put it on a saucer on the kitchen window sill.
It's smaller than the palm of my hand,
dome shaped, soft and bright green.
It drinks it's own weight of water every day
and I've taken to calling it Brian.

A couple I once knew gave names
to their outdoor clothes, particularly scarves –
Are you going to wear Maureen to the shops?
– until they had children and became sensible

I've never named a plant before.
While I'm away from home I'm hoping
he's coping without me.

I Could Kill that Bloody Dog

We are thick with wildlife near Tower Bridge,
squirrels trying to bury nuts on our balcony
and building dreys in our BBQ,
tapping on the windows when they're hungry,
and that's just for starters.
Foxes! They leap the fences to get to us,
peer through the windows at night with lamplit greedy eyes
and mangy with hunger.
Herring gulls off the Thames line up on our roof
drowning us out, worse than Heathrow, and crapping everywhere.
What are we, a soup kitchen?
But the hedgehogs are usefully omnivorous
and enjoy all the poo, from whomever.
Speaking of Heathrow, we have incoming ducks landing.
I suppose they are wild – they aren't house trained.
I do admit to throwing them a crust or two,
the ducklings are sweet.
And then of course there are the usual feral cats
and sewer rats and mice who move in
with their luggage and thirty five babies.
Moles pop up between the flagstones.
I won't even start on the wasps, we can hear them
chewing up our new wooden window frames for their nests
which are like something from a 3D printer. Unreal.
Speaking of unreal, there are the occasional wallabies
that can leap the fence. And they're not even natives.

M40 to M42 to M5

We turned off the roaring motorway
and the helpful hectoring sat nav
relaxed into quiet as we drove slowly
along narrow known roads.

Cobwebs draped the Old Man's Beard
in the hedges and dripping skeletal trees
lined the lanes, stark against the sky.
And there was no more 'heavy traffic ahead'

only the distant red lights of a tractor
glowing briefly at a bend ahead
and turning off at Evan's farm.
Nearly home then.

This is an Announcement

Arriva Rail Wales Ltd apologises
to our customers for any inconvenience
caused by the cancellation of the 07.32 to Crewe
due to an unforeseen incident between Hereford
and Leominster.
This was beyond the control
of Arriva Rail Wales Ltd.
There will be another Crewe train
arriving at platform 2 at 09.32.
Please speak to the station staff
if you have any questions.
Please stay calm.
Arriva Rail Wales Ltd are sorry for the delay
which is beyond our control
and for the inconvenience to our customers.
Thank you.

But if any other of our customers
are thinking of throwing themselves
in front of a through train to Crewe
please bear in mind that it will
inconvenience themselves,
their fellow passengers,
and Arriva Rail Wales Ltd. Thank you.

Garden Cows

Last night, in muffling snow, four cows
flipped their gate and wandered up our lane.
The only witness to their venture were the owls
and me. No-one complained.
Alerted, barking dogs were crossly hushed
when cattle blinked at sudden safety lights.
They blundered, clumsy, slipping on mud and slush
innocent intruders, meaning no harm, at night.
They looked for things they'd like to eat
and licked warm-tongued at statuary, pots and stones
to no avail. Garden plants were brown and bitter-sweet
and when they'd searched in vain they headed home.
I wish they'd return, friends from my day-lit world,
moon-shadowed, strangers on my hoof-holed verge.

Marmalade

There's a pot of your dark orange marmalade in my cupboard,
still unopened. It lasts a long time but I might never open it now.
The last time you gave me some jars I asked how much
you'd made and you said enough to see us out.

You could have meant for that year's breakfasts, maybe you did –
we shared that phrase as we got older. It used to make us laugh.
It was an excuse for my very expensive superking mattress and
the hard-wearing twill you bought to cover family wing chairs.

You gave me a blue jug for tulips, wide rimmed and perfect
for allowing that slow graceful spreading as they die.
I gave you a metal garden bench which was given back to me
painted grey, a two seater, where I'll sit when it gets warmer.

This year I've twice filled your blue jug with white tulips for you.
I've glued your last card on the wall – we sometimes sent the same
card to each other, unknowing. Things that last, we liked,
things we both loved and which have seen you out.

The Local Park

Gobbets of grey snow
around the park's rim
cloak dog turds and fag ends
but also emerging snowdrops
to be revealed by spring.

My Friend the Prize-Winning Poet

Of course I had to say I was delighted for her.
In fact be the first of us to say it.
I didn't think it necessary to mention
that I too had entered the competition.
Of course I smiled and smiled
and said I loved one particular line
in her winning poem – the last is a pretty safe bet
but I hadn't actually read it
and I won't be fucking reading it either.

Landing

on water
is the tricky part.
You must slow down
almost to stalling speed
finely judged.
You've then to calculate
the length of the waters
(the depth is immaterial).
When you lower your undercarriage
is a matter of experience –
your speed dictates
how fast and how far
to walk on the water
before folding your wings
and hoping nobody saw you
as you glide away, swanlike.

Acknowledgements

Thanks to the following publications where some of these poems, or earlier versions, first appeared: *Clear Poetry, Ink Sweat & Tears, The North, Nuggets and Nutshells, Acumen.*

'Aldermaston March 1962' was first published in *Noble Dissent*, edited by Rebecca Bilkau (Beautiful Dragons, 2017).

'Recollected in Herefordshire' was first published in *A Bee's Breakfast*, edited by Rebecca Bilkau (Beautiful Dragons, 2017).

'Awake at Night' and 'The Best Medicine' were first published in *The Emergency Poet*, edited by Deborah Alma (Michael O'Mara, 2015).

'Today's Headlines' was first published in *The Everyday Poet*, edited by Deborah Alma (Michael O'Mara, 2016).

'Second Person Personal' was first published in *#MeToo* (FairAcre Press, 2015).

'The Best Medicine' was also published in *The Poetry of Compassion*, edited by Patrick Pietroni (University of New Mexico Press, 2019).

Thanks to Joy Howard and Grey Hen Press for first publishing several of these poems in *Looking Over My Shoulder at Sodom* by Meg Cox (Hen Run, 2014).

None of the above would have happened had it not been for my friends Marilyn Francis, Jenny King, Pru Kitching, Jayne Arnott, Lesley Ingram, Christine Stibbards, and Jean Atkin.